T0065180

ENDORSEMENTS

"A masterful take on how a trauma-informed human being made it from teacher to superintendent. Humbling personal story."

Dr. Lora De La Cruz, deputy superintendent,
Boulder Valley School District

"Insightful and easy to read, the book reminded me of my own personal story and my professional career from teacher to superintendent."

Dr. Martha Salazar Zamora, superintendent,
Tomball Independent School District

"Danna uses her own life story to show us how we can achieve our dreams no matter what obstacles come our way. Inspiring."

Eva Bonilla, community leader, Fort Worth, Texas

"I have known Danna for many years, and I have seen her go through her personal and professional trajectories in life. Danna exemplifies the impact of how important it is to own your personal experiences and serve as an exceptional leader. Life was not easy for her, and she made it from the projects in Harlem and high school dropout to obtaining a doctorate and serving as superintendent of schools. I am proud to call her *hermana*."

Richard Carranza, former chancellor of
New York City Schools

"All will learn and be inspired from this powerful sharing of life obstacles and challenges but staying resilient. Dr. Diaz is a shining example of how education can be your passport to success."

Dr. Michael Haggen, chief academic officer, Scholastic

Servant Leadership
MY JOURNEY FROM TEACHER TO SUPERINTENDENT

*7 Principles to Guide Women Educators
on Their Path to Success*

Dr. Danna Diaz

ARCHWAY
PUBLISHING

Archway Publishing books may be ordered
through booksellers or by contacting:

Archway Publishing
1663 Liberty Drive
Bloomington, IN 47403
www.archwaypublishing.com
844-669-3957

ISBN: 978-1-6657-4640-3 (sc)
ISBN: 978-1-6657-4641-0 (e)

Library of Congress Control Number: 2023912095

Print information available on the last page.

Archway Publishing rev. date: 8/30/2023

I would like to dedicate this book to my mother, Ines Montalvo, and daughter, Jasmine Ines McCormick. They have been my rock throughout my journey, and I would not be writing this book if it were not for them.

Contents

Preface

Dear Reader:

Thank you for picking up my book for a little inspiration. I decided to write this book because I was told that I would not be a good teacher when I was in college. And when I was a teacher, no one ever told me that I would be a good administrator. I decided to pursue my administrator certificate because I wanted to make a difference. When I was an administrator, I did not know that I would have a doctorate and become a superintendent. And even though it took me fifteen years to get my first job as a superintendent, I did not give up.

I do not want you to give up.

Because I went through so many experiences that compelled me to move forward and upward, I knew I wanted to make a difference in the lives of students and families. I know I want to make a difference for you!

If you are a college student and thinking of becoming a teacher, this book is for you.

If you are a teacher and thinking about being an administrator, this book is for you.

If you are a teacher and administrator thinking about getting a doctorate, this book is for you.

If you are an administrator thinking about becoming a superintendent, this book is for you.

I wrote this book so that I can share what I went through. I know I am not the only one, and I know you have your own chapter to write and your own story to tell.

I figured if I share my story, you will feel inspired and motivated to move on and accomplish your goals. I know I did, and I create new ones all the time.

I also hope you are motivated to write your story and share it with others. There is so much to learn in life, and there are so many people who can be inspired by your story.

Every time I have an opportunity to share, I know I am making a difference.

May you reach your dreams, meet your goals, and make a difference in the lives of others.

God bless, and thank you.

Acknowledgments

This book would not have been written without the support of my husband, Carlos Torres. I would also like to acknowledge my two coaches, Pat Alva Kraker and Lisa Randolph. All three played a big role with this book, and I would like to acknowledge their contributions.

Introduction

This is my story on how I transitioned from one experience to another in education as a teacher, principal, central office administrator, and superintendent. The autobiography demonstrates the resilience, perseverance, hard work, integrity, organizational and leadership skills, and how being the first in many positions and initiatives allowed me to have a trajectory full of encounters that are heartwarming, soul-searching, tear-jerking, and funny. The narrative gives a glimpse of the personal and professional practices that fueled my courage to be brave and risk taking in the transitions I took from one experience to another. I hope each reader finds wonder, solace, and encouragement knowing that they have similar events and discovers new ideas to move forward in their own personal and/or professional capabilities.

I know I am not a rare commodity, and we all have similar happenings, but it was important for me to write it down and share some things that helped me make it through life. This book is intended for women in leadership positions serving in education and educational administration. The book focuses on my personal and professional life as a student, classroom teacher, principal, central office administrator, and superintendent. Along the way, I learned the value of resilience, perseverance, hard work, organizational skills, and integrity. These character traits have been invaluable to me in my journey. You will find a chapter on leadership and a chapter on my firsts. Being the first Latina in several positions also added to my story. The events I share in my story may strengthen your desires to grow professionally and catapult where you want to go in your career.

Growing up, I did not know I was poor. I loved school. I experienced trauma at a young age, and through every transition in my life, I problem-solved my way out of situations and ensured I had support through life. And most importantly, I navigated the bumps and barriers that got in the way.

My hope for you is that you learn a few things throughout this book. Whether this book gives you affirmation or confidence that someone like me can go from being a high school dropout to obtaining a doctorate and serving as superintendent of schools, I would like for you to take a few nuggets of what I have learned. Through my story, I will guide you through a path that will help you meet your goals. Education, training, and learning are a way of life, always asking the question why, finding solutions to problems, and knowing who is there to support you. And lastly, removing the barriers to get stuff done.

The first chapter of the book will explain my personal journey. I will move from there to explain a few lessons I learned to build resilience and perseverance. Then I will describe why it is important to keep your word and how I learned about hard work from my mother. Next, I will give you some samples of why it is important to be organized when you begin something and how important it is to finish it as well. It is related to integrity not just with people but with yourself. Then I will share some tips I learned on leadership and most importantly as being the first Latina and/or the first in implementing an initiative.

Through my book, you will learn the values that got me to where I am. If you bring these principles into your life, you will get there.

I believe that you can accomplish anything if you set your mind to it. You can maximize opportunities by finding a solution and finding out who is on your team. Know that you will hit some curves and bumps, but that is life. You will make it through as long as you remember that anything is possible. You must plan, be patient, and move forward.

My hope for you is that you will see many similarities and be encouraged to take the leap on the next trajectory in your life. I encourage you to stay strong and positive. My intention for you is to get clear on your journey as a female leader and accomplish your professional goals. My story will help you get there.

Chapter 1

Building My Resilience: My Early Years

I learned my resilience from my earliest years. I was born on October 28 at the New York Infirmary in New York City. This hospital was founded by two strong women, Elizabeth and Emily Blackwell, who were sisters, in May 1857. They wanted a place where women could learn about medicine. I share the history of the hospital where I was born because I grew up being supported by women and learned how to support women. I believe where I was born adds value to who I am today.[1]

I lived on Delancey Street on the Lower East Side of Manhattan. My mother worked in a factory, sewing blouses, and my father was a baby food distributor. Our apartment was too small for our little family so my mother applied for housing and was able to move to the Grant Projects on Amsterdam Avenue in Harlem.

Grant Houses is a public housing project at the northern boundary of Morningside Heights in the borough of Manhattan.

Morningside Heights Inc. (MHI) was founded by Columbia University and other area institutions to begin renovating Morningside Heights to target the "undesirables" and stop neighborhood blight. MHI helped lobby for slum clearance in the 1940s with the intention of using the legislation to displace residents on the fringes of the neighborhood to keep the area middle-class. From the beginning, the project bore the stigma of its racial agenda. The *New York Times* noted the racial identification of the first five families to move into the Grant Houses: "two white, two Negro and one Puerto Rican."[2]

I am sharing the history of where I was raised so that you understand how I experienced societal racism at an early age. This experience is important to note due to my personal and professional experiences and what I had to endure to build my own resilience, perseverance, problem-solving, hard work, and organizational skills. In addition to being the first Latina in some of my experiences and how this experience shaped who I am today.

It is important that I share with you that I have an older sister, and she has a different father. She is half Puerto Rican and half Jewish American. She is seven years older than me and lived with us in Harlem. Her name is Darlene Cohen, and her married name is Darlene Levy. Even though I do not share much about her in this book, it is important for you to know that I have a sibling.

School Experience

I attended New York City Public Schools in Harlem, started kindergarten and first grade at Public School (PS) 125, and transferred to PS 36. PS 36 was the first school in the city to be built for only kindergarten through second grade; most elementary schools were for kindergarten through sixth grade. PS 36 was built as a partner school to nearby PS 125 to help enroll some early childhood students, since PS 125 was becoming too crowded. I attended second grade at PS 36.

PS 36 was named in honor of Margaret Douglas. She was the granddaughter of a slave and grew up in Washington, DC. She won a four-year scholarship to Howard University and graduated in 1922. She earned her master's degree from Teachers College, Columbia University, in 1938, and took other courses at City College, Hunter, and New York University. She started teaching at a Harlem elementary school and became assistant principal at PS 10 in Harlem. In 1949 she was named principal of PS 133 in Manhattan, only the third African American to become principal in the NYC school system. Her school was listed as "one of the best five in New York City" in 1957 by a survey by the State Department of Education. Then she became principal at PS 129. In 1960 she was the first African American woman assistant superintendent in the New York City Public Schools, and she oversaw District 19 in Brooklyn. In 1967 she became the first African American woman deputy superintendent in charge of curriculum for the New York City Public Schools. She worked for forty-four years in the New York City Public Schools.[3]

Why am I sharing the history of the school I attended? Because it was in second grade that I knew I wanted to be a teacher. I played teacher and had invisible students.

This book is intended for women who want to make a bigger impact in their professional careers or have the same trajectory as Margaret Douglas and me: teacher, principal, central office administrator, and superintendent. I was also the first Latina in many of my positions as principal, central office administrator, and superintendent. It is impactful to learn that the school I attended was named after a woman of color who had the same trajectory and was the first in many of her positions.

Faith

A fond memory I have from living in Harlem is my faith. My mother raised me as a Catholic, and we attended St. Joseph Catholic Church in Harlem. It is a Black Catholic parish church on 125th Street. I attended Sunday school, and I did my first communion at the age of seven. I've always known I am a child of God and that he is always with me. My faith keeps me humble.[4]

Family Trauma

The interesting thing about my personal journey is the trauma I experienced at a young age. The incidents developed my resilience and made me stronger.

When I was seven years old, my dad came home one night beat up with black-and-blue eyes. My parents always tucked me in for bed, and that night, he explained that he fell off the roof. I am not sure if what he told me was true. I will never know the truth. All I remember is that my life changed. My life changed because my mother decided to send me to Puerto Rico. I learned that my father was a drug addict.

At the end of my second grade, my mother sent me to Puerto Rico to live with my aunt. My mother told me that the reason she sent me to PR was to be able to leave my dad; he was deep into drugs, and she did not want to see me suffer anymore.

What I remember about living with my aunt is that we lived in Rincon. I remember that they had an outhouse. I attended school for a short time, and I cannot remember the name of the school because I was traumatized. Why and how did I experience trauma? The transition from moving from NYC to Puerto Rico. Feeling a sense of abandonment from my parents and not knowing why I was left to live with my aunt. You would have thought that trauma would not be something I would experience as a young child; however, I learned over the years that trauma is part of life. Again, building my toughness and tenacity. My resilience was being built time after time.

Soon thereafter, I moved in with my maternal grandparents in Mayaguez, Puerto Rico. There I was enrolled in third grade at Federico Asenjo Elementary School, and I was immersed in the Spanish language. I recall walking to school and stopping by the bakery to buy sweets. I studied and excelled in school. My grandparents' neighbors' children shared their notebooks from the previous school years, and the notebooks were verbatim what I was learning the current academic year, which made learning easy even in another language. Living with my grandparents was a wonderful experience. I remember taking a taxi, wearing a uniform, and all the other good things that came from going to school. I studied every day and ensured I received good grades.

The most important things that I can recall are some traditions in our culture. We had a small farm where we had coffee, bananas, oranges, and all the good food we ate at the kitchen table. We raised chickens and pigs. I remember picking coffee beans, drying them outside, and hand-grinding the coffee beans. I also remember when we would slaughter the pigs for festive meals and kill a chicken for soup or to eat with rice. It was hard for me to eat the chickens since I would feed them and give them names. My grandfather would have to go to the supermarket and buy chicken for me to eat since I did not want to eat the chicken we raised. I also remember how important it was to take naps. We took daily naps and when we woke up, we would drink a cup of coffee with milk and Boricua bread. Yes, I started drinking coffee at an early age. It was tradition and it still is.

While I was in Puerto Rico, I remember my mother and father coming to visit. He was high on methadone and was in bed most of the time. My mom would visit with family, and my dad could not engage in any conversations due to his addiction. I always wondered why she left me to live with my grandparents. There was a sense of abandonment, and this feeling allowed me to build my resilience because I adapted, remained positive, and continued to study in school.

My grandfather owned a hardware business, and it was located next door to my grandparents' home. My grandmother would cook every day. My grandfather sold everything in construction from plumbing supplies to construction materials. He stored many of the materials near the farm.

I had a traumatic experience at a young age, and what I remember is that I did not feel comfortable in Puerto Rico anymore. I remember telling my mother that I wanted to move back to New York. At the end of fourth grade, I made the move back with my mother and lived in a one-bedroom apartment in the Bronx.

Moving Back to New York

I was excited to be back with my mother. The only thing that was different was that she was living with someone else, and his brother lived there as well. I did not know who my stepfather was, and I felt a sense of resentment toward him. Who was this man living with my mother? It was not my father. It was a strange feeling. I remember being angry and rebellious. I believe there was also a sense of betrayal.

I attended PS 11 on Ogden Avenue. I did like school, and I loved my fifth-grade teacher. I was placed in a bilingual program because I was speaking and reading Spanish fluently. The schools in Puerto Rico did a great job teaching me literacy and numeracy. My friends and I had a crush on our teacher. I remember doing well in school and passing fifth grade.

At the home front, my mother's absence made me lonely. She worked at a factory sewing blouses for the wealthy. My stepfather worked at a jewelry store. I remember being a latchkey kid and hanging out with friends who were not the best influence. I was a rebellious kid, adjusting to the new life in the Bronx. My resilience was being developed.

I attended Junior High School 80 in the Bronx. I do not remember much of that experience because I was traumatized at home. I attended school and hung out with friends at the park by the school. I do know I changed. I had friends and was influenced to join a gang, the Junior Ghetto Sisters. I would skip school, and I remember going to a park because the Senior Ghetto Sisters were going to be in a rumble. All I remember is that we never made it because one of the sisters was killed on the train tracks. She was electrocuted. I thought, *I do not want to die.* I was in complete shock when I learned what happened to someone so young. This time of my life is a blur. Trauma is real. I was smart enough to know that being in a gang was not a good choice. The good news is that I moved from the neighborhood.

My mother bought a candy store on 163rd and Morris and we moved to the apartment above it. My mother decided to quit her job at the factory and work full time at the store. Soon thereafter, she bought the deli next door and made the deli and candy store a bodega. The name of the bodega was Raymond's Grocery Store. I changed schools and started to attend Roberto Clemente Intermediate School 166. I remember liking school again, and I loved math. The school was a block from the bodega, so I walked to school.

One of the most traumatic stories I remember is when my sister was trying to get a hold of my father because she had not heard from him in a while. She wrote him a letter and it was returned stating deceased. We found out my father died a month after he passed. He was homeless and died of sclerosis of the liver. The hospital already buried his body since no one claimed him. I heard that his family was trying to raise money to give him a proper burial but that never came to fruition.

There I was, a young teenager with no father. Although I did not have a long-lasting relationship with my father, I remember when I was young and how much I loved him. When I learned that he died, I was sad. It created a void in my heart.

As a teenager, I continued to build my resilience and had the opportunity to work in my mother's bodega from time to time. I worked after school and on weekends. I loved to eat candy. I brought snacks to school and shared with my friends.

In school, I was promoted from eighth grade, and I attended the eighth-grade graduation ceremony. My grandfather came from Puerto Rico to celebrate, and my sister's best friend, Alma, also came to my graduation. It was a special occasion.

What I did not know then is that it would be my only cap and gown graduation until I graduated from college. You see, although I knew I loved school and I had a desire to be a teacher, my trajectory was not traditional.

Teenage Years

During my freshman year, I worked in my mother's bodega, and I learned my father died. I attended Taft High School in the Bronx (one of the most troubled schools in New York City). I was truant my freshman year and failed all my classes. Why? I hung out with the wrong people and all we did was cut class. I also think that it had a lot to do with the trauma I experienced at a young age and learning about the loss of my father. I did not have guidance or positive influences to show me the boundaries I should follow. I created my own. At the time, I did not know what a bad influence was. I just tagged along because I thought it was cool.

Moving Back to Puerto Rico

I believe that the reason I was sent back to Puerto Rico was because my mother sold her business in New York and we were transitioning to a new life.

My mother sent me to live with my grandfather, and at this time, he was living with his mistress. I attended Jose De Diego High School in Mayaguez. I was enrolled in a bilingual program where I took classes in English and Spanish as a sophomore. Suddenly, I was making A's and B's and was having success. It took my mother a few months to sell the store and send her belongings to Puerto Rico. She rented a small house while she built her new house on a piece of land she purchased. Then, another tragedy happened. My grandfather fell ill and died. Another void in my heart.

The two most important men in my life were gone. What's a girl to do? Well, I received permission from my mother to get married. I believe I wanted to get married because I wanted to get away from living with my stepfather. I had to get out and build a life for myself. I experienced too much trauma and believed that getting married would be the best thing to do. At the end of my sophomore year, I planned a wedding, and I was married at the tender age of fifteen. Soon thereafter, I moved to Fort Hood, Texas.

As you can see, all these stories from my early life to teenage years developed my life of resilience. The trauma that I experienced was real. I exhibited grace and a positive outlook, although there was trauma through every trajectory in my early life. We all have a story to share, and I know my early life events created the woman I am today.

Questions to Think About

What is your story?

What did you go through?

How did your experiences shape who you are today?

Chapter 2

Developing My Perseverance

Moved to Texas

My childhood experiences gave me the resilience I needed to persevere. At the tender age of fifteen, I planned a wedding, moved to another state, and lived on my own. Yes, that was me, and yes, I did it!

In Texas, I enrolled at Killeen High School as a junior. Then, three months after I was in school, I became pregnant. When school personnel found out, they did not want me to attend the traditional high school and placed me in an alternative high school for pregnant girls.

The school was across the street from where I lived. I remember feeling a sense of isolation. I did not want to read "Beowulf" and decided to drop out. It was evident that the curriculum was not relevant to me, my culture, and what I was going through.

During this time, I was going through a lot personally. The day I gave birth to my beautiful daughter, I was alone. My daughter's name is Jasmine, and she was born on May 20, 1977.

Did I persevere? Yes, my daughter gave me the courage and determination to continue with life as a dedicated mother. She was born healthy, and I was ready to be a mom.

At a young age, I was trying to figure out how to balance my life as a mother and wife. I wondered if I was living a normal healthy life. My daughter's father was given orders to move to Germany, and I moved back to Puerto Rico while he found us a place to live. I went to live with my mother in her new home in Mayaguez. I was sixteen with a beautiful baby girl, and we lived in PR for six months.

Moved to Germany

In December 1977, I moved to Karlsruhe, Germany. We lived in government housing for soldiers and their families. I was a stay-at-home mom for the first eighteen months of my daughter's life, and then I decided to go to work. I am not sure if I was restless or just wondering what kind of life I could have for myself and my family. I applied for a food service worker position.

I worked in the mess hall where all the soldiers had their meals. I worked eighteen months and decided to take a class on effectiveness training for women. In the class, I learned to be assertive and to accomplish the things that I wanted by taking action and setting goals. I applied for a motor vehicle dispatcher position and decided to go to night school to obtain my high school diploma. I also applied for a motor vehicle driver position that paid $13 an hour, and I got the job. It was a grandfathered position, which meant I could have the job for life. This was the beginning of my independence and determination.

At the tender age of twenty-one, in Karlsruhe, Germany, I received my high school diploma from Big Bend Community College, Moses Lake, Washington. I was so excited that I knew I could go to college and accomplish the things that I set my mind to do.

During this time, things were not working out for me personally. I decided to leave Germany and move to Puerto Rico. I left all my personal belongings behind. My daughter and I moved in with my mother, and I started to look for universities to attend. What I realized is that the systems at those institutions were too slow. One school registration took over eight hours. Then I consulted with my sister, and she asked me to move to New York. She knew someone who needed help in an attorney's office. So, I went to NYC and started to work as a secretary in a law firm. When the attorneys asked me how much I wanted to get paid, I stated $200 a week in cash. In 1981, I am not sure if that was the going rate, but I felt good about it. The attorneys were surprised at my ability to manage the office and provide bilingual services to clients. As determined as I was, I knew I was going to make it. My perseverance gear kicked in, and there was no stopping me now.

At that time, my daughter's father showed up at the attorney's office and asked me to go back to Germany with him. I refused. Then I thought about it. I knew deep down inside that if I stayed in New York, I would be working and would not be able to get my education. In New York, it is all about the hustle of work. There would not be any time to slow down and get an education. I knew I had to make a difficult decision. I compromised. I told my daughter's father if I went back with him, we would move back to the United States so that I could go to college, and he agreed. So, I moved back to Karlsruhe, and in the fall of 1982, we moved back to Fort Hood, Texas. I enrolled at the local community college in January 1983 and started my education career to learn how to be a teacher.

Going to College

I know there have been many times that we have to go back and forth to ensure we make the best decisions for our children, and I believe deep in the bottom of my heart that moving back with my daughter's father was the best decision I could have made so that I could go to school and get an education.

Not only was I a good student at the community college, but also my Spanish professor asked me to teach Spanish at the female prison. She knew I wanted to be a teacher and gave me the chance. Was I scared? Yes, but I knew I could not turn down this break. This opportunity taught me how to be vulnerable and humble and at the same time teach creatively.

I visited the nearest four-year university and documented the courses I needed to acquire a bachelor's degree. I ensured that all my credits from the community college would transfer to the four-year university. I attended both the community college and four-year university at the same time. By 1985, I graduated with an associate degree, and in 1986, I graduated with a bachelor's degree. Did I persevere? Yes.

Let me tell you why. I had to, because around that time, it suddenly seemed like everything was falling apart. I was attending two institutions of higher learning, my daughter's father and I divorced, my grandmother died, my house was vandalized, and my supervising teacher told me that I would not be a good teacher because I did not know how to speak English.

I had to move from where I was living and find a place for my daughter and me to live. I had to apply for government assistance for rent, utilities, etc., and my daughter qualified for free and reduced meals at school. In order to make some money, I started to participate in work study at the university. During these setbacks, I was determined to succeed. Nothing was going to stop me from achieving my goal of becoming a teacher. I knew I had to continue and finish. There were many obstacles in the way, and I continued to remove them and find a way to achieve what I needed to accomplish.

Becoming a Teacher

When I graduated with my bachelor's, I decided to move to Houston, Texas. I became a substitute teacher, and at one of the schools, the assistant principal was a great ally who helped steer me toward a path that would help me advance in my career. She informed me of a full-time job for the upcoming fall semester. The state gave me an emergency certificate for bilingual education, and I started to teach first-grade bilingual students at Franklin Elementary School in Houston ISD. The assistant principal, a Latina leader, informed me of a program for teachers to receive their bilingual certification. I visited the University of Houston-Clear Lake, and another Latina leader, Dr. Andrea Bermudez, explained the program, set up a meeting for me to meet the Dean, and by January 1988, I was enrolled in graduate school. My second year of teaching, I had the honor of receiving the Distinguished Bilingual Teacher of the Year award from the Houston Area Association of Bilingual Education. If only my supervising teacher from the university could have seen me receive the award!

As a single, working mom, I was attending graduate school and ensuring not only that I would achieve my dreams but also that my daughter attended a good school. I made it! Living the dream! Persevering through it all.

What I realize now is how I continued to persevere no matter what people said I could not do. I showed them that I can. I worked hard and ensured that I made it.

The experiences that I had while I attended college were experiences that usually more mature women experienced. At the age of twenty-four, I was divorced, and by the age of twenty-seven, I was working as a single mom and attending graduate school. My trajectory was not traditional, and by the time I finished graduate school, I was twenty-nine years old. Not bad for a high school dropout from the Bronx.

When we persevere, we can be scared, and we must take these opportunities. We also must acknowledge and recognize when other women open doors for you. It was a common thread for me, women helping other women.

I succeeded because I persevered. Think about a time when you persevered against all odds to accomplish something.

Questions to Think About

What changes happened in your life?

How did you persevere?

Where can you open the door for other women?

Chapter 3

Keeping My Word-Integrity

Graduate School

Integrity is the quality of being honest and having strong moral principles. In my previous chapters, I explained how I developed my resilience and perseverance. In this chapter, I am going to explain how I learned and developed my values and at the same time stayed true to myself and family.[5]

While I was working as a teacher, I learned right away that I wanted to be a principal, especially because of the way parents were being treated in the office. Parents were being treated unfairly, and I wanted to advocate for Latino families. I personally knew the challenges I experienced as a child, and my personal experiences allowed me to have empathy for families I served in the public school. I researched the coursework I needed to pursue my midmanagement certification and enrolled at the university to continue my graduate studies. I also decided to work for the amnesty program at the community college and worked two jobs. As a single mom, not only was I able to fulfill my responsibilities as a mother, but I also continued to work and study to ensure I followed my passion.

As a teacher, it was important to plan, design lessons, and create formative assessments to ensure students were learning the standards. Consultation with families was also important and they knew how to help their children at home. Parents knew they could come to me with any question, activity, or concern. Why? Because their child mattered to me, and they knew it. Every time the students took the state assessments, they exceeded and were above grade level in math and reading. Having integrity with students, families, and colleagues led to outstanding outcomes.

Multilayered Level of Growth with Integrity

I navigated work, graduate school, and motherhood with strong principles. I attended all parent teacher conferences, helped my daughter with fundraisers, and ensured she had what she needed to continue her education. As a graduate student, I paid my own tuition, studied with my colleagues, and moved up the ranks at my workplace. I was able to serve as grade level chair, site-based decision-making committee, and lead teacher. In addition, I taught all grade levels at the elementary level in seven years of teaching. At the community college, I moved from English as a second language (ESL) teacher to payroll supervisor. In order to move from one grade level to another and one school to another and to get the positions I received was because I kept my word and had the integrity. I walked the talk and talked the walk. Having integrity is important.

After completing the midmanagement certification program, I was able to move to an assistant principal position. A colleague from my graduate program reached out to me and opened the door. Another woman of color opened the door and gave me the opportunity to apply for an administrator position. My first assignment was at an elementary school, and I remember the superintendent and assistant superintendent being supportive. They asked me to serve as the bilingual coordinator as well. They ensured I received training in leadership development. They were open to new ideas and supported the creativity I brought to the district. Not only were we able to start a dual language program at one of the schools, but we also provided multicultural education and diversity professional development to the entire district.

As a young girl, I did not know even know there was a college in my neighborhood, until a professor from Columbia University was killed in front of my elementary school. At the tender age of seven, I learned that you could go to college and become a teacher. The sad news is that I learned about college from a tragic event. Because of this experience, I knew that I had to ensure that the students I served knew that there is a college in their neighborhood.

For this reason, I created a College and Me program for fifth-grade students whereby they took their classes at a college campus. This work entailed detailed planning and commitment. For this reason, I was tapped to go to the middle school as an assistant principal to help with student outcomes for our male students of color.

During my time as an assistant principal at the middle school, I designed programs for our male students with professionals who were interested in investing time to our youth. It was important to provide role models and demonstrate possibilities for students who might not otherwise be aware of them. Students learned about engineering, football, clinical psychology, and community engagement. In addition, I periodically worked with the teaching staff to ensure students' academic learning was being met so that students could succeed. I am proud to say that in a year, the student outcomes went up by double digits. An increase in academic achievement was evident in statewide assessments. At LPJHS, the school moved from low performing to acceptable in one year. Scores increased for students in seventh-grade reading for African Americans from 44 percent to 58 percent; for Hispanics from 67 percent to 78 percent; seventh-grade math for African Americans from 22 percent to 48 percent; for Hispanics from 56 percent to 69 percent. Eighth-grade scores for African Americans in math went from 25 percent to 60 percent, and Hispanics from 37 percent to 70 percent.

Having served middle school briefly, I can attest to this: anyone who can survive, much less thrive, in this environment can indeed do anything.

Becoming a School Level Administrator

I remember going to a district office in La Marque ISD, La Marque, Texas, and the human resources administrator looked at me and stated, "You are what we are looking for." I was hired as a principal right away, and I was excited to be the first Latina principal. I am not sure if district personnel knew why it was important to have a Latina administrator as the principal. I know why it is important. The key for the district was to hire someone qualified. For me, it was to be a role model and demonstrate how being a Latina role model makes the difference in student outcomes. Again, my first year, I worked with teachers and ensured students had what they needed to learn, and in a year, student outcomes went up by double digits. At Inter City, an increase in academic achievement was evident in statewide assessments. In third-grade reading, scores improved for African Americans from 72 percent to 87 percent; Hispanics from 88 percent to 100 percent; third-grade math scores for African Americans from 59 percent to 71 percent; for Hispanics from 77 percent to 100 percent; fourth-grade writing for African Americans from 56 percent to 75 percent; and in fifth-grade reading for Hispanics from 87 percent to 100 percent.

How did we meet these outcomes? I was able to give teachers planning time to create lessons and collaborate. They were able to be creative with schedules and lessons. Families and students knew that as a school we cared about them. We provided family engagement opportunities where parents learned what their child was learning at school. Students were excited about school. There was a student council, and students had a voice. They even petitioned to have a Valentine's Dance. I asked the students to write a detailed plan for the dance, and it was approved. Success at the school was evident, and the school was number two in achievement in the district.

As a single mother and with my daughter attending Syracuse University, I had to change jobs to make more money. I moved to Austin, Texas, to serve as principal. I cried when I saw the building because it looked like a prison with a nine-foot fence with barbed wire. I started to meet staff and learned there was a significant division between staff and families. I collaborated with team leaders and implemented team-building activities, ensured traditions and customs were honored, and provided high-level professional development. I am proud to write that at Brooke Elementary, from 1997 to 1998, Hispanic students' scores were as follows: 45 percent to 60 percent in third-grade reading and 36 percent to 62 percent in third-grade math. And 100 percent of the students passed the Spanish test in the third-grade reading and math. In fourth grade, the scores were 67 percent to 85 percent in reading and 76 percent to 81 percent in math. At Brooke, I met with students to set goals. They were able to analyze their own data and determine their areas of strengths and opportunities. Individual students created goals and an action plan on how they would meet their goals. I also collaborated with teachers, and we designed a professional development plan that improved how we implemented instruction in the classroom. Our professional development was on the weekend, and they were compensated for attending. Not only were they compensated, but also, we provided meals for our staff.

The results of the students' assessment data demonstrated that both teachers and students worked hard to accomplish their goals. Brooke Elementary was 100 percent Hispanic, and 100 percent students experienced poverty. I remember my area superintendent coming to visit me at the school when the state assessment results came out and I was the first school he came to visit. He asked, "How did you do it? How did you increase achievement by double digits?" I stated, "It was the students, families, and teachers. They deserve the credit."

When you have strong values and integrity, students, staff, and families know that they mean a lot to you as a leader. We ensured that our values and beliefs were aligned with the organization's values and beliefs, and for this reason, student outcomes always improved during my tenure as a teacher and principal.

I was visiting a friend in Florida and was asked to apply for a principal position. The area superintendent interviewed me while visiting Austin. Another Latina opening the door. She stated I would have to interview with the school team, and I did. I was hired and moved to Orlando, Florida, to work at Orange County Public Schools. I served at Little River Elementary School. I was their first Latina principal, and an increase in academic achievement was evident in statewide and national assessments from 1998 to 1999. Florida Writes scores moved from 2.9 to 3.0; FCAT fourth-grade reading moved from 296 to 299; fifth-grade math moved from 298 to 312. SAT scores improved from 44 to 52 in reading and 58 to 60 in math. How did the scores improve? By collaborating with teachers and giving them the time to plan out lessons and formative assessments.

However, there was something else that I experienced: overt racism. Brown and black students were treated differently from white students. English learners were pulled out of instructional lessons from their teachers. If students did not have money, they would not eat lunch. The cafeteria staff did not have someone assigned to clean tables and sweep the floors, and it was discouraging to see how students of color were being treated. I worked in the cafeteria every day cleaning tables and floors. I also paid for the students' meals. The area superintendent and superintendent knew what I was experiencing, and it was evident

I experienced macro- and microaggressions, including implicit bias at the school.

I knew then what I know now. If I became a superintendent, I would not allow racism to happen in my district. I was naïve of course. I did know that although I passed my superintendent certification in 1999, no one would hire me. The glass ceiling was low. I consulted with my area superintendent and let her know that I would have to leave Florida and go back to Texas to pursue my PhD. I was honest and continued to go for what I valued the most: to learn more so that I could get better at my craft in educational administration.

Another Transition

I returned to Texas, and I was able to get a job in Round Rock ISD (another woman interviewed me for the job and opened the door) and I applied for the PhD program at the University of Texas at Austin. My daughter graduated from Syracuse University, and she moved back to Texas. When I consulted with her about pursuing my PhD, I asked her if she was going to stay in school and get her master's. She he stated, "Mom, I plan to go to work." So, I knew that I could go and continue my education.

Starting My PhD Program

Out of sixty students who applied to the PhD program, only fourteen were selected, and I am proud to say that I was. I started my PhD in the summer of 2000, and it was an adventure. I learned new vocabulary, and some courses seemed foreign to me. But thanks to my resilience, perseverance, and integrity, I was able to pass all the exams, take all the courses, and complete the program in four years.

What I know now is that in my early years, I attended four elementary schools, two middle schools, and four high schools, and as a teacher, I taught in four school districts. I was also a principal in five school districts. I attended four institutions of higher learning. History repeating itself, however, I was learning and growing every time.

There were so many experiences that helped me with my perseverance, resilience, and integrity. Every opportunity sharpened my saw to be a better leader.

Questions to Think About

What transitions did you experience?

How do you live with integrity when life throws you transitions?

As an educator, how do you keep moving despite the circumstances in your life and get positive outcomes?

Chapter 4

Organizational Skills

Doctoral Program

When I was an assistant principal, my supervisor wrote me a note that stated, "Your organization, hard work, and willingness to take initiative, love for children, and sense of humor have earned you such respect as an administrator, as a person, you deserve an A+." What I learned during my doctoral program is how to be more organized. Not saying that I was not organized before, but I learned many different skills that I needed to learn to sharpen my saw with my organizational skills. Taking different courses and exams in the program allowed me to organize my time so that I could earn good grades. Throughout my program, my GPA was 3.8. I only received two B's in the entire four years.

When I started the doctoral program, I was working at Round Rock ISD and decided to resign from my position to be able to focus on my studies. I was able to be off for a while and then applied for a position at the Region Education Service Center XIII in Austin. It was a position titled governor's initiative education specialist, and our department was responsible for the Texas Reading Initiative. We trained Region Education Service Centers staff across the state so that they could implement the new reading initiative in the twenty regions. In addition, we were responsible for the Commissioner's Conference on Student Success. We organized all the conference materials, workshops, lunches, and dinners. Event planning became a full-time job. I sharpened my organizational skills not only with this position but also with my courses at the university. I also had the opportunity to work as a consultant and assist schools that did not meet adequate yearly progress. The consulting gig allowed me to use my organizational skills at two different school districts and ensure student achievement increased at both schools.

I was determined to earn my doctorate so that when I would apply for superintendent positions, my application would be placed on the maybe or yes pile for an interview. You see, I was certified as a superintendent in Texas in 1999 and knew that I would have to earn my doctorate to get an interview. Sharpening my saw meant being as organized as I could be to understand how to be an educational leader responsible for an entire system. Although I earned ninety credit hours for my Doctor of Philosophy, nothing prepared me for the superintendency. It took years of different positions in different districts to understand the complexities that it takes to lead a system.

First Central Office Position

In 2004, I graduated with my doctorate, and I cast the net out wide. My first regional superintendent position was in the

School District of Philadelphia. Another woman of color gave me an opportunity and opened the door. I drove from Texas to Philadelphia and found a beautiful apartment to rent on ninth street. The landlords were amazing, and so was the former tenant. I lived in the Italian area of Philly and the Italian market was a block away. I lived and worked in a beautiful place.

I was responsible for the South Region and loved serving the principals and staff. My district office was on sixth street, and I could walk to work, especially on snow days. What I learned in this position is the influence of trauma in the community and how it impacted schools. In my first week on the job, there were five deaths, a student was in the wrong place at the wrong time and was shot, two families were impacted by murder-suicide, and the partner of one of the directors had a heart attack. When I called my mentor, he stated, "This is the work of the school executive. You must learn how to manage trauma along with everything else in the district." I did not know that this would be something I would experience. It was not covered in my doctoral program, and I did not experience it in other districts that I served as a campus principal and teacher.

That year, I also learned about boundary changes, family engagement in culturally specific neighborhoods, and how to work on capital projects. Lastly, community organizing and charter schools were also very active in the district that I served.

As regional superintendent, my newly honed organizational skills kicked in. I hired a new executive assistant and a new director of student support services and ensured that we continued to provide customer service to the schools. We changed how we held our principal meetings, and the principals wanted to host the meetings at their schools. We signed up to ensure we were equitable in the process. We collaborated with the University of Pennsylvania to ensure we were designing data-driven decision-making at our feeder pattern school meetings. Our boundaries were changed to ensure students were attending their neighborhood schools. I met with phenomenal community leaders who taught me the importance of organizing. Most importantly, I worked with fascinating regional superintendents in the district. What I remember the most is the importance of staying organized with all the processes and deliverables that the regional office was responsible for.

With the expanded opportunities and experiences, however, came additional challenges. There were some other politics playing in the game. You see if you are not from the city or area, you are treated differently. I experienced those differential treatments with regional superintendents from the area and me. Particularly if they were men. You see, I do not play politics—or as others call it, *politricks*. If I am hired to do the work, then I do it. My tenure in Philly was short, and I will always cherish the lessons learned.

Texas Positions in Higher Education and Central Office

I decided to move back to Austin, Texas, and chose to start searching for central office positions. I began to work at Austin Community College as an adjunct professor teaching preservice teachers in a special populations class. I was grateful to continue my profession as a professor. As you know, when you teach, you learn.

During the fall of 2006, I interviewed with two school districts: Port Arthur ISD and Fort Worth ISD. Although Port

Arthur was offering me $10,000 more in salary, including social security contributions, I decided to move closer to family and accepted the director of student engagement position in Fort Worth ISD. I know that it was the best decision at the time because my daughter was married in 2004 and moved to Plano, Texas. My grandson was born on October 31, 2006, and I moved to Fort Worth in December 2006. God had a plan, and I thank him for the opportunity to be closer to family.

I would like to thank Aracely Chavez for noticing my application and giving it to the hiring manager. Another woman of color giving me the opportunity. On my first day of work, she invited me to attend the Hispanic Women of Texas, Fort Worth, chapter event. I was able to meet wonderful Latinas who welcomed me with open arms and became my tribe.

I also served on the education committee, served as a board member for the Rose Marine Theater (Latino Theater), and after graduating from Leadership Fort Worth, I was elected to serve on the board. I also served on YWCA board and began anti-racism work with the organization and school district. What I was not able to do in Philadelphia, I was able to do in Fort Worth. Community engagement was a game changer. I participated with the Industrial Areas Foundation local interfaith group and was nominated to take the residential community organizing training in Chicago.

Serving as a central office administrator was important but so was learning how to enhance my skills with community engagement. I provided districtwide professional development in academic acceleration, student leadership, and school completion to campus personnel. I provided leadership in the research, implementation, and monitoring of the Children's Defense Fund

Freedom Schools Programs in the summer 2012 and planning for future programming at the district and community level. I was the coleader and facilitator for the Family and Community Engagement Community Action Team—Morningside Children's Project, a University of North Texas and Fort Worth ISD collaboration. I collaborated with the Fort Worth, Houston, and Fort Worth chambers of commerce and district personnel to implement a districtwide Prevail to Graduation Stay-in-School Walk from 2008 to 2012. Because of my leadership, over nine hundred volunteers visited four hundred homes. I created Community Action Teams (CAT) and collaborated with stakeholders in the community involving approximately 1,500 stakeholders engaged in planning meetings, community forums, CAT meetings, etc. With all this engagement and with my organizational skills, there was an increase in the graduation rate.

While I was working with the school district, I had the opportunity to serve as an adjunct professor for Tarrant County College and teach preservice teachers for a couple of years as well as serve as an instructional coach for graduate students at the University of Texas at Arlington. I coached in the business finance, school law, and superintendent courses. I did so well that I was asked to be an adjunct professor and was able to teach graduate students who were interested in obtaining their superintendent certification. You know I had to be organized to not only have a full-time job, serve as a board member in community organizations, and teach in higher education. It became a masterpiece for me to be able to manage all my responsibilities with grace. The good thing is that I was ahead of the game teaching hybrid and online courses. I learned early on what we were going to ask teachers to do in the future. I had a hunch that if I learned how to teach online and hybrid, I would understand what teachers would have to go through as a district leader, and I am glad I did. While I am writing this chapter, we are in a pandemic (COVID-19) and our teachers had to pivot to online and hybrid learning, something I did fifteen years ago.

Leadership Academies

One of the things I love to do is learn. During my time in Fort Worth, I participated in several leadership academies to develop my leadership skills. I participated in the Association of Latino Administrators and Superintendents (ALAS), Superintendent Leadership Academy (SLA), California Association of Latino Superintendent Association (CALSA) Mentoring Program, Center for Courage and Renewal Leadership Academy, and Leadership Fort Worth. Every one of these academies developed my skills, and I met wonderful people at the local, state, and national levels.

One of my colleagues from the ALAS and SLA was hired as superintendent of El Paso ISD. It was a district in need of improvement, and it was sanctioned by the state. He asked if I was interested in helping him with the work, and I consulted with my family. They agreed that I should, and I applied. I asked him where he needed me the most, and he stated as area superintendent. I was hired and served the Bowie, Coronado, El Paso, and Jefferson-Silva feeder patterns. I worked with amazing principals. We had to ensure we followed all internal audit reviews, allowed for creativity and innovation, and at the same time ensured we increased student achievement. Working in El Paso taught me how to improve my organizational skills for a district that needed system improvement. I had several meetings with families regarding transfer and discipline appeals, many human resources meetings regarding personnel issues, and school visits to conduct instructional rounds. In addition, I attended all the board meetings. It was a busy time. What I learned about being at El Paso was that there were so many systems and processes that needed to be improved. Furthermore, I learned that I worked too fast for some and was a bit direct for many. The good news is that I did the best I could. The superintendent knew that I would be looking for a superintendent position.

Questions to Think About

What organizational skills did you develop?

What organizational skills helped you with your work?

Chapter 5

What My Mother Taught Me about Hard Work

---------------------------------- ⌘ ----------------------------------

Modeling Hard Work

One of my students contacted me fifteen years after I taught him and asked, "Are you the Danna Diaz that taught at Helms Elementary?" I said, "Yes." I was working for Fort Worth ISD as director of student engagement. He stated, "I am J. D. Hinojosa, and I was in your fifth-grade class." I stated, "Yes, I remember you. Did you change your name?" He explained why he changed his name. I was so happy to hear from him. He told me about his work and family. One of the things that stuck out the most was when he said, "I wanted to contact you because you were one of the teachers that taught me about hard work. Remember the saying 'Students will not remember what you taught them but how you treated them.'" He remembered how I modeled hard work.

At Helms Elementary, I was teaching a multiage fourth- and fifth-grade class. As lead teacher, I acted as the assistant principal. I also organized many family engagement programs. This is the kind of job I was doing when I made such an impression on this student. I remember receiving Teacher of the Year too. What did that mean? Although I was one person, I did the job as though I were three, and I did not even mention serving as a social worker as well. I believe in all my seven years of teaching, I served in several roles going above and beyond the call of duty to get the work done.

I learned about hard work from my mother. She worked in the factory, and she was a business owner. I would see her work fifteen hours a day to bring food to the table and to make sure we had a roof over our head. My mother only had a sixth-grade education, and she made it. I knew that with hard work, I would make it too.

This chapter is about the experiences that I had going above and beyond the call of duty and how hard work was evident in all the positions I had as a teacher and administrator. You will get a sense of how I worked hard and see the similarities and differences of what hard work means to you.

Hard Work as a Teacher

I worked hard all my life. Working long hours, mastering the skill at hand, and ensuring all tasks were completed on time. I remember as a teacher I had to make sure all my student folders were completed with correct information on assessments, discipline, etc. I was always the first teacher to turn everything in. At the end of the school year, I submitted all my books and prepared my classroom for the summer. I was always the first to finish. I was always the first to be at the school a week early to get my classroom ready before school started. Hard work was part of my DNA. It transferred with me when I became a school and central office administrator. Every single detail as a classroom teacher (e.g., lessons plans, formative assessments, family meetings, report cards, and team meetings) was part of the work of a teacher. Every day was different and rewarding.

Hard Work as a School Level Administrator

As a school level administrator, not only was I responsible for ensuring student learning was at the forefront of instruction, but I also ensured that professional development was relevant to the teachers. As a principal, I learned about the responsibility of facilities and how it was important to work with contractors.

The other part of school level administration is when community partners use the building. I became a facilities planner. Again, wearing more hats at the school level. The work of a school level administrator entailed planning staff meetings, professional development, evaluation of staff, managing a budget, ordering supplies/materials for teachers, contracting with consultants, reviewing lesson plans and report cards, ensuring classrooms were covered with subs, student discipline, family engagement planning, and collaborating with other principals in the district. The list goes on.

Hard Work as a Central Office Administrator

As a central office administrator, the roles became more adept. I became an ambassador for the school district. Serving principals and community partners and adding other affinity groups. For example, working with civic, faith, and business leaders was another layer of relationship building. This does not include all the community service work I did. Again, working above and beyond the call of duty to get the work done for the students I served. As a central office administrator, I learned how the system worked or did not work, and I had to create systems to be aligned with the organization. I collaborated with many stakeholders to get buy-in on district initiatives. I ensured that professional development was aligned with the district initiatives. I wrote grants and managed budgets. I managed several projects and ensured all stakeholders were engaged.

Hard Work as a Superintendent

As a superintendent, there is even more to do. I had to do all the aforementioned and then some more. It all depends on the needs of the community. Then I backward and forward plan. This time, I had to implement strategic planning in the toolbox and ensure the voices of the community are heard. I implemented program reviews and/or audits so that we had a benchmark of the work that we needed to move forward. I ensured I had a way to access data so that I could make data-driven decisions.

This time, not only did I have to focus on student learning and professional development, but I also had to add strategic planning, financial planning, system improvement, capital projects, research and accountability, and state and regional engagement to the mix. You talk about managing the demands as a CEO and at the same time ensuring all aspects of the work are organized and planned accordingly. Again, serving different roles and going above the call of duty.

My mother always taught me that there is one key to success, and it is hard work. She was proof that the American dream is real and that with hard work you could get anywhere. My mother came to the mainland from Puerto Rico with almost nothing. She worked at the factories, and with a sixth-grade education, she became a business owner. She passed her DNA hard work to me. I am a first-generation college graduate. Through my graduate programs, I worked two jobs and was a single mother. With hard work, I graduated and changed positions to get the promotions I needed to raise my daughter. It was my duty to work hard and carry my mother's success forward.

Questions to Think About

What are some examples of your hard work?

How did hard work impact what you do as a person and/or professional?

Chapter 6

Leadership

My leadership journey has been with me since my high school career. I served as the secretary for the bilingual education program at Jose de Diego High School in Mayaguez. Moving forward, taking leadership roles has been a part of my life. In college, I was the treasurer of the Texas Student Teacher Association. As a teacher, I became a grade-level chair in my second year of teaching, and the leadership roles continued with the building site-based decision-making committee, family engagement coordinator, etc.

What I learned about leadership is having influence with colleagues who do not report to me and are there for the same mission and goals so that as a team we can accomplish what we set our minds to do. The mindset of being a servant leader is very important because service for others is a blessing not only personally but also professionally. What I would add to the leadership journey are shared accountability and delegation. Over the years,

I learned how we delegate and hold each other accountable for the things we agreed we would accomplish as a team.

I am going to go deeper into the things I learned over time regarding leadership in this chapter. I hope these lessons I learned will help you in your journey. The most important thing is the legacy you will leave behind. How are you going to leave the organization better than you found it? What will continue when you leave?

Influence

When I started this leadership journey, I did not recognize the influence I had with other people. I developed the ability to recognize my talent of being an influential leader when I worked with groups of people to accomplish a project and we were able to celebrate the success together after the plan was completed. Being an influential leader takes time, trust, relationship building, and respect for one another. What I learned with experience is the importance of developing the relationships with internal and external stakeholders so that they know your why and purpose. Once they see you in action, they state to themselves, "This is someone I would like to work with."

I will give you an example. In Fort Worth, when I served as director of student engagement, my role was to engage the community so that they support the superintendent's goals. I met one-on-one with community members and asked if they would be interested in serving on the community action team. When I had my first meeting, we had over forty people from eight affinity groups: business, faith, social service agencies, parents, students, teachers, higher education, and administrators. We met and created action plans to accomplish the superintendent goals. We planned college summit events, professional development opportunities for social service agencies, and community and neighborhood walks to bring students back to school, and we implemented community-based reading programs in the summer and after school. I also worked with all the high school student advisory councils, and they all developed and implemented projects that were student created and led. Influence is being able to accomplish the task at hand with people who do not directly report to you. I can tell you that the faith community is still implementing a summer reading program today because of the work we did together.

It is very important to work with someone who has vision. As a leader, I embraced the vision and followed through. There was a specific vested interest by the superintendent; I learned to bring different facets of the community and leave a legacy.

Servant Leader

What I love about my leadership journey is that I learned that I exist to serve people. I owned my work as a work of service. Not wanting anything in return. I always wanted people to feel good when they were around me and knowing that I would keep my word with the things I said I would accomplish. I always tried to be kind and honest.

There are so many examples I can give you about being a servant leader. In Fort Worth, I remember working with high school students and Habitat for Humanity. I would organize weekend work projects with students who were interested in serving. I would register the team, schedule transportation, and organize meals for students. We would meet at the location and work for eight hours on a Saturday to help build a home for someone in need. This was not only demonstrating servant leadership but also modeling for students how we continue to serve the community in different capacities. I believe that all the work I do is to serve humanity and leave the world a better place for all of us.

What I believe I taught the students is that servant leadership is a leadership philosophy in which the goal of the leader is to serve. Instead of the people working to serve the leader, the leader exists to serve people.

Shared Accountability

Working in a team at work or in any group, it is important to have a system of shared accountability so that nothing falls through the cracks. Have you ever built a Lego before? You have the pieces and a book, and you start building by following the instructions, each piece fitting in and scaffolding the pieces until it becomes a masterpiece. Shared accountability is an agreement with a team to accomplish a project, and little by little, the conceptualization of the project is built until, alas, it is completed. Each member of the group holds each other accountable through the process until the project is done. Most of the time, projects will be seamless, and other times, there will be some storms that you must navigate based on trust and relationships. The key is to remember your why and purpose. Refocus, recharge, and keep going.

Delegation

If you haven't noticed already, you will realize that most of your leadership journey will be delegating to people you work with or serve. It is having a high level of trust and respect to get the goals accomplished. Most of my work is done by delegation. The inarguable rationale for delegation is there is no way I can complete all the work that needs to be done on my own. I have learned to delegate and trust that the work will get done, knowing that no one is perfect, and we will make mistakes. The key is to keep moving on with continuous improvement and project plans.

I learned as a leader to delegate not to micromanage because you will not get the work done. I learned early that I do not need to control every part of the project. I discovered I had to trust the process and my team.

Legacy

Leaving a legacy is an interesting aspect of a leader that does not always come up. I think the point is partly that good organizational systems will be robust and self-perpetuating to an extent. What is the legacy you will leave behind? How are you going to leave the organization better than you found it? In Fort Worth ISD, the summer reading program continues, and I left in 2013. In San Juan Island School District, the elementary school has a fire suppression system and the high school locker rooms were remodeled during my tenure. I remember telling the custodian at the elementary, "Just look up and remember me. The fire suppression system will save the building and most importantly save lives." At Reynolds School District, hiring more librarians, counselors, and social workers will be my legacy. In my tenure, we never laid anyone off and we were able to lower class size. At Reynolds School District, I worked with the legislative members to get funding for a school-based health center. It was built in 2020. Today I am proud to say that the center is a sample of the legacy I will leave at Reynolds. Leaving a legacy is important.

Leadership is one of the most important roles you will have in life. Whether it is at home, work, or your faith, it is important to remember that you must influence others, serve others, and leave the organization a better place.

In the next chapter, I will take a deep dive in my leadership roles as the first Latina. You will find yourself being the first at something. Someone will remind you or you will realize it. The key is to make a difference in the lives of others.

Questions to Think About

What is the leadership legacy you will leave behind?

How are you going to leave the organization better than you found it?

Chapter 7

Being the First

Being the first in my family to graduate from college and being the first in my family to earn a doctorate was a big undertaking. Throughout my career, I found myself being the first to do something, such as a project, a plan, or an idea, as a Latina. For example, when I received Distinguished Teacher of the Year, I was the first to receive the award in only the second year of teaching. In addition, I was the first to receive Teacher of the Year twice from the same school district. When I reflect on the awards I received, it was because of my students achieving at high levels and the family engagement I coordinated at the schools. I want to encourage you to be a trailblazer and not to be afraid of doing something new.

Administrative Career

When I started my administrative career, I was hired as the first Latina assistant principal at a school district and was responsible for the bilingual program and cultural diversity training as well. Again, I started a College and Me program where fifth-grade students attended college for a week. Again, first of its kind in the school district. I continued this initiative at other districts that I served to ensure students had an opportunity to learn that there was a college in their neighborhood. Why? Because I knew that I wanted to be a teacher and I did not know there was a college in my neighborhood until a crime occurred in front of my elementary school. I wanted students who were marginalized and experiencing poverty to know that they too could go to college and there was an institution of higher learning not too far from where they live. This initiative was done when I served La Porte ISD, La Marque ISD, Austin ISD, Orange County Public Schools, and Round Rock ISD. What I know now is that I made a difference for the students I served, and I worked with a great group of community members and teachers to help me pull it off.

Facing Racism as Being the First

When I became a principal, I was also the first Latina principal in La Marque and in the school I served in Orange County Public Schools. As a central office administrator, and first Latina serving as director of student engagement. As superintendent, I was the first Latina for both positions. One of two Latinas in the state of Washington and Oregon.

It was eye-opening how I experienced overt racism in most of the places where I worked. I always thought, *If I am experiencing racism, I know our students and families are too.* I believe my perseverance was key to getting by in a situation where racism is endemic. I believe my legacy helped reshape attitudes positively.

First to Implement an Idea

In Fort Worth, I was the first to implement Children's Defense Fund (CDF) Freedom Schools, and in Oregon, the district was the first to implement CDF Freedom Schools. In Washington, I was the first to bring people of color as keynote speakers and Latino students to train staff on implicit bias and stereotypes. Why? It was important to bring culturally relevant summer programs for students of color, and it was important for staff to see people of color in different settings. In Friday Harbor, I had an idea to bring Dolores Huerta to showcase her documentary. It was only an idea. I brought the right people to the table, and it was the first time in the island's history we had a Latina to come and speak about her social justice work. I heard repeatedly, "It was a great event. I never saw the theater so full." I know I did not do it alone. Anytime I was the first in implementing something, it was always in collaboration with a handful of community stakeholders who also believed in the vision.

Being the first is not easy. I am in a fishbowl. Everything I say, everything I wear, and anywhere I go is being observed. I tell you this story because it is OK with being the first. The key is to remember the way you do it. Always do it with quality and excellence, and always invite the right people to help you pull it off.

Don't be afraid to be the first. This is part of your legacy.

With being the first come consequences. You have to have thick skin and remember people will criticize you. Stay strong!

Questions to Think About

What experiences or roles did you have where you were the first?

How did those experiences influence you as a leader?

Conclusion

This book was intended to give you some inspiration and learn how I overcame challenges that you may face in your life. I hope you were able to take some nuggets with you.

My hope for you is that you continue to learn, grow, and remove obstacles that get in the way. Remember that anything is possible.

Please remember that when you feel you cannot do it, you have strong resilience, perseverance, organizational skills, integrity, hard work, leadership, and your experiences as being the first at doing something new or being the first in the position. You will make it through and accomplish your goals.

Don't forget to share your story. You made it! Now make a difference in someone's life!

I truly appreciate you.

Endnotes

1   https://www.britannica.com/place/New-York-Infirmary-for-Women-and-Children.

2   https://en.wikipedia.org/wiki/Grant_Houses.

3   https://ps36margaretdouglas.com/our-story.

4   https://www.stjosephsharlem.com/saint-joseph

5   https://www.google.com/search?q=integrity&btnK=Google+Search&sxsrf=AOaemvJxtmntE6f_CiigkX9F1vvWlZhtPg%3A1630416152005&source=hp&ei=Fy0uYYD6Ocry-wSJ95OoBw&iflsig=ALs-wAMAAAAAYS47KMZ26N0nFL7s-mTprJFWIJ7LT3Lp.